SOCIAL GRACES

MANNERS, CONVERSATION, and CHARM FOR TODAY

ANN PLATZ
and SUSAN WALES

Illustrations by KATHRYN ANDREWS FINCHER

HARVEST HOUSE PUBLISHERS
EUGENE, OREGON 97402

Social Graces

Copyright © 1999 by Ann Platz and Susan Wales

Eugene, Oregon 97402

ISBN 0-7369-0112-4

Artwork designs are reproduced under license from Arts Uniq', Inc., Cookeville, TN and may not be reproduced without permission. For information regarding art prints featured in this book, please contact:

Arts Uniq'
P.O. Box 3085
Cookeville, TN 38502
1.800.223.5020

Design and production by Koechel Peterson & Associates
Minneapolis, Minnesota

Harvest House Publishers has made every effort to trace the ownership of all poems and quotes. In the event of a question arising from the use of a poem or quote, we regret any error made and will be pleased to make the necessary correction in future editions of this book.

Printed in Hong Kong.
99 00 01 02 / IM / 6 5 4 3 2

Contents

Minding Our Manners

*E*ven in this hustle-bustle world, manners and courtesy still have their place. Whether you are visiting in a friend's home or being interviewed for an important job, your etiquette will tell more about you than your words ever will. Minding our manners is one of the simplest lessons we'll ever learn, yet it takes most of us a lifetime to master. It's basically common sense. Be kind to others, be respectful, and be careful to treat others in the way you most desire to be treated. Social grace is one of the basic keys to experiencing happiness and giving others happiness in return.

Today, amidst all the advances and miracles of the modern age, we tend to lose sight of each other. In the last century, especially, our focus has communally shifted to the experience and the needs of the individual. From fast food drive-throughs and pay-at-the pump gas stations all the way to automatic cash machines, we have worked increasingly hard to limit our interactions with each other. It is no wonder that we have lost sight of how to behave and how to treat one another. Undoubtedly, today's manners, or lack of manners, would raise our grandparents' eyebrows. I (Ann) can just hear my grandmother asking me what I'm trying to get away with. It doesn't work that way, I hear her saying to me.

My friend Susan Wales and I wanted to write *Social Graces* because, as Southerners, we were reared on the importance of good manners. I grew up in the low country of South Carolina in a town by the name of Orangeburg that lay about seventy miles north of Charleston. I spent my childhood in our wonderful family home known as "Willbrook," a large farm that belonged to my grandparents before it was passed down to my father. Politics, quail hunting, low country cuisine, and Charleston manners were the order of the day.

My father was by profession a lawyer and a state senator and by birth a gentleman farmer. I first learned protocol from his knee. He was of the old school where manners counted! My mother was the perfect politician's wife, allowing her genuine warmth and social grace to flow to everyone she met. She also saw that her children knew their manners and always wrote their thank-you notes. You can argue the nature v. nurture theory all day long if you want, but the truth of the matter is that I came by social grace as if it were born into my blood. It is a special gift from my parents to me. I was also blessed with a grandmother who stood over me to correct my grammar and encourage me further in the social graces.

It was because of my parents' engaging and hospitable nature that Willbrook was always bustling with people of all ages coming and going at all times of the day. Daddy encouraged what he called, "Late night, short-order" meals. He and mother would entertain our group with his childhood and courtroom stories and her travel stories and recipes.

Clara, our family cook, was like a second mother. She would come over and cook fried chicken, eggs, and grits.

Everything, anything, even in the middle of the night, if we begged. No matter what time it was, we always had delicious food and lots of good times and storytelling punctuated with peals of laughter.

At Willbrook, the house policy was that there was always enough room for one more person even if it meant scrunching together at the kitchen table, and that there would always be a warm plate heaped with Clara's famous cooking. Oh, these were happy times.

I have carried these same values into my adult life and have often entertained my guests with stories of my childhood and family. I now pass these memories and tales down to my grandchildren with love and care. Today, as an Interior Designer, my calling is to find the beautiful in the midst of the mundane. Etiquette is nothing more than discovering the beauty that is internal. It is a kinder, more genteel, way of living and relating with others.

When I met Susan Wales nearly twenty years ago, we experienced instant friendship. Susan has always been more of a sister than a friend to me. Over the years since, we have laughed, cried, prayed over problems, and talked for many, many hours on many, many topics. *Social Graces* is born out of our friendship and our commitment to living a gracious life.

Kindness is always fashionable.

AMELIA E. BARR

We chose *Social Graces* as the title of our book for several reasons—primarily because of the many definitions of the word "grace" itself. Grace comes from the Latin word, *gratia,* which means to favor or to charm. Over the years, it has come to mean everything from a charming personal trait and virtue to divine assistance and the sanctification of man. Social graces are the tools necessary for unearthing the beautiful. It is our hope that you carry from this book these same definitions of grace. We firmly believe that the social graces will deliver you into a state of grace—a state in which kindness begets happiness and personal joy becomes an infectious gift you share with others.

As I work with clients, I combine my background and thoughts on etiquette and manners with discussions on lifestyle. I have explored the possibilities of effortless beauty and easy elegance in my clients' lives. So, writing this book is a culmination of years of this dialogue. And I have found that in teaching them the lessons I have learned in my lifetime, they have taught me so much more.

When Ann Platz and I met, I knew I'd found a lifelong friend. Both daughters of the South, we shared similar views about what Ann calls *the art of beautiful living* . . . known to most as good manners!

Good manners touch every aspect of your life. Perhaps you are up for a promotion or maybe you're going to meet your fiancée's parents for the first time or maybe you are graduating from college and going into the world of business. Whatever the reason, you have the desire to improve your manners and your lifestyle. This book is for you.

Hardly anyone who grew up in the South escaped a lesson in hospitality and manners! That was certainly true in my hometown of Roanoke, Alabama where I not only learned social graces from my family, but in the fifties and sixties, everyone felt responsible to ensure that children were on their best behavior at all times. A forgotten, "Yes ma'am" or "thank you," was quickly corrected by the adult ear that caught it.

It was considered a rite of passage for a young girl in the South to receive a book of manners from her mother, and I received my first on my tenth birthday. At the same time, I was assigned the chore of setting the table. I learned to fold napkins in a variety of ways and to line the silver beside the plates with military precision! Sunday dinners were my favorite when mother would ceremoniously bring out the dishes from the tall china cabinet and bring in camellias from our garden for our table.

As I endure the hectic pace of my life today in Los Angeles I often dream of the social graces that filled my childhood. In the cool breezes of summer afternoons long ago, family and friends would glide gently in the old-fashioned swings and rockers by our lake. I can just taste the cookies still warm from mother's oven and hear the tinkling sound of ice in her lemonade pitcher. Memories of my father's famous neighborhood barbecues in our backyard come to mind as I recall Mr. Peek from next door cutting into ice-cold watermelons.

The book of manners given to me by my mother at that tender age was just the first that she would present to me throughout the years. I count the social graces and my faith instilled in me by my parents the most precious gifts of my childhood.

"An etiquette book . . . huh?"

My husband, Ken, teased me that he should keep me under lock and key for at least a year after the book comes out. "Are you prepared to become an example? Everyone will be watching you," my husband joked.

"No problem," I assured him. "My parents taught me beautiful manners!"

"What about the time you reached across the table and speared the chocolate strawberry off the top of my chocolate mousse at the Beverly Hills Hotel," Ken reminded me.

"Maybe this etiquette book's not such a good idea after all," I told Ann.

"Nobody's perfect all the time, and everybody wants to have better manners," she replied. "Not to worry."

I certainly wasn't worried. Well, at least not until Ken and I attended a large social event where I sat at the table with the guest of honor and a host of other celebrities and dignitaries. Unfortunately, Ken volunteered that I was writing an etiquette book. I wanted desperately to kick him, but he was across the table and out of reach. I can assure you that the glare this Southern belle gave him could have stopped the entire Union army from crossing the Mason-Dixon line.

The focus of the dinner completely changed. They studied me, watching my every move, checking to see which fork I used, which spoon I chose. Then they began firing questions at me: "What should I do about this or that?" I was pleased. Ann had been right. There is always room for improvement and people are open to learning. I gracefully rose to the occasion and radiated confidence as I triumphantly led my table through a crash course in manners. Everything was perfect, until I cut the artichoke heart in my salad and it flew off my plate into the lap of the guest of honor.

"Do as I say," I jokingly announced to the horrified dinner guests at my table, "not as I do." (That's why we've included how to recover from faux pas in our book. After all, no one is perfect . . . especially not me.)

Both Ann and I were single mothers during a season of our lives where duties were overwhelming. Therefore, we have great empathy for those who "do the best they can with what they have." Sometimes just providing for your family is all a mother, father, or grandparent can do. *Social Graces* is dedicated to all of you and is our special gift to you. Now you have Ann and Susan in your lives . . . just refer to us as your Aunt Grace! As you study this book, consider how you can apply these principles to your life. We can assure you that you will live life more abundantly, and in turn, make the world a better place!

Ann's the decorator and Susan's the gourmet and hostess. We both love to entertain and will give a party at the drop of a hat. We make a terrific team and have lots of advice to give.

Be sure to listen carefully to everything your Aunt Grace tells you, and you might just learn something. Here's your first lesson: Don't sit next to us at dinner, unless of course your napkin is covering your lap for protection! We hope you enjoy our book!

CHAPTER ONE

Hospitality

"WHAT DO YOU MEAN YOU'RE NOT SOUTHERN . . . ?"

*S*ocial graces are your invitations for others to come inside your world. Throughout American history, Southerners have lived a polite, genteel way of life. Their friendly and cordial ways have endeared them to those they meet. For instance, in Charleston, South Carolina, if you are strolling down the street and you see a gate partially open, it means that you may enter and enjoy the garden. In other parts of the country you could be arrested for trespassing if you dared to enter someone's private property. But not in the South.

We believe the charm and the legendary status of southern hospitality has remained one of the constants in American culture. Immortalized in fiction and movies, and now the latest, in web pages over the internet, good, old-fashioned southern charm is as uniquely American as apple pie and cotton candy, yet as distinctly regional as cheese grits, Brunswick Stew, fried chicken, and Virginia Ham.

> *It was easier to do a friendly thing than it was to stay and be thanked for it.*
>
> LOUISA MAY ALCOTT, *LITTLE WOMEN*

Perhaps one reason for its lasting reputation is that the South is the land of tradition. Generations ago, life was observed from the viewpoint of the front porch—preferably from a tall wooden rocking chair. Conversations began and hours passed. As young children, we remember rocking on the porch after supper with our parents and our grandparents until the sun gave way to the chirping of the evening crickets. In the days before television, family stories were passed in comforting voices from relaxing parents and grandparents in wicker chairs and hammocks to the sleepy ears of children.

When you are on the receiving end of these, you feel both loved and cared for. Our traditions of grace and charming hospitality lie at the very heart of southern culture. Social grace is the South's enduring quality and most unmistakable trademark.

Visitors to the South expect to be greeted with a big smile, southern drawl, and large glasses of iced tea. Why shouldn't they? It's a reputation that wasn't created by accident. Everyone knows that Southerners are renowned for their hospitality. Not everyone, however, knows to what extent Southerners will go to ensure their visitors have a truly memorable experience.

In September of 1989, my parents hosted two Russian women with the Friendship Force in their home. At the same time, Hurricane Hugo came roaring through South Carolina with full force. There are not many things in this world, either natural or man-made, that can keep a southern hostess from the duties of entertaining. When the lights went out, my mother simply lit candles and continued with the meal as if it were what she had planned from the beginning.

The morning after the storm, my mother greeted her guests with towels and bars of soap and a somewhat unusual offer. The Russian ladies were invited to go to my brother's house for a refreshing post-hurricane bath in his swimming pool. The electricity was out for three days, so she cooked the food that was thawing in the freezer on the barbecue grill. The guests were so enchanted by their southern hostess that when they returned to Russia they sent her a thank-you note stating, "Your hospitality was stronger than Hugo!"

The lesson from this story is that a good hostess will always look for special ways to make her guests feel cared for and appreciated. Quite often it's the tiniest details that do this. A truly great hostess is one who is able to think and act quickly to effortlessly problem-solve in the midst of even the most overwhelming difficulties.

In these socially challenged times, the South still shines as a true role model when it comes to grace, charm, and hospitality. It is the land of perpetual social engagements, from modern-day afternoon teas to checkered tableclothed picnics, from the world's best barbecue to fried chicken. It's the place where social poise and prominence are still admired above all else and your great-grandmother's china and special silver pattern have never gone out of style. Perhaps it is the intense heat, coupled with the humidity, that have slowed us down. Southern hospitality is famous for elegant candlelight dinners, outdoor barbecues, and Sunday afternoon meals with cool mint tea and hot biscuits. The South remains to this day the land of decadence and extravagance when it comes to the rules of society.

A close friend once shared the story of how her family introduced their future son-in-law to their Thanksgiving festivities. We include this story because, although it's important to keep your cool when hosting, it's also imperative to keep your sense of humor. Being able to laugh at your situations and yourself is an important part of social grace.

Carolyn and Joe were preparing for the first visit of their future son-in-law. It was Thanksgiving, and with their four daughters coming home to Florida for the holidays, it was a busy time.

Carolyn chose a recipe that required the turkey to cook at 500 degrees for one hour. Then the oven was to be turned off and the oven door was to remain shut until they were ready to carve the turkey the next day. It seemed like a flawless recipe. As Carolyn prepared the extra-special menu, Joe prepared for his serious talk with Casey, the intended son-in-law.

Carolyn cleaned the house, polished the silver, and ironed her best tablecloth and napkins. Tired, she laid down for the hour the turkey was to cook. The ease of the turkey preparation was a blessing in her busy schedule.

At six o'clock the next morning, Joe awoke to the horrible smell of something burning. He walked into the kitchen and peeked into the oven to find a very burned turkey. He nudged Carolyn awake.

> *But the fruit of the Spirit is love, joy,*
> *peace, patience, kindness, goodness,*
> *faithfulness, gentleness, self-control.*
> THE BOOK OF GALATIANS

"Oh my goodness . . . look at that turkey!" she half laughed. It was charred. Then it hit her. "What in the world am I going to do?" she panicked. "Dear Lord, You are in the redemption business. Please redeem this turkey," she begged. As she pleaded, Joe began to scrape away at the burnt areas of the turkey, only to reveal a perfectly smoked breast intact and not the least bit dried out!

The house was being aired out and fans were busily humming as Carolyn rallied the troops, "Girls, we've had a little disaster, but we're going to stay in control. Do not laugh or giggle about the turkey. Today is Carol's day. Remember, everything is going to be fine. Let's keep this disaster our little secret." Carolyn sprayed perfume on all of them to cover the smell.

When they sat down for Thanksgiving dinner, eyes darted back and forth. Joe blessed the hands that had prepared the food. Carolyn smiled.

Casey tasted the turkey and said, "This smoked turkey is great! It's delicious." With this, Carolyn let loose the laughter she was trying to hold in. Everyone else started laughing. Carol and Casey were clueless. Carolyn finally confessed the story of the redeemed turkey and welcomed Casey into their family!

One of our most beloved passages in the Bible discusses what is called the Fruit of the Spirit. Love, joy, peace, goodness, faithfulness, gentleness, and self-control, remain etched in the memory as the epitome of social grace. Social grace isn't just knowing which fork to use. It's about finding confidence in the knowledge that, come what may, you will be fit to handle any situation with poise, tact, and, most importantly, grace and love.

I (Ann) remember well the wonderful English hospitality my husband and I received during our visit to the enchanting English estate, Somerly. After a lovely dinner with our host and hostess we returned to our bedroom. Our hostess had our bed turned down for the evening and had placed a hot water bottle in the middle of the bed underneath the sheets. I can't begin to tell you how wonderful the warm sheets felt. As I slipped beneath the covers, I forgot entirely about the chilly evening outside the windows. Under my pillow, she had placed a fragrant packet of dried flowers sewn inside a handkerchief. I slept like a baby that night. Our hostess had seen to everything, and all the charming and thoughtful touches let us know that she really valued our visit as well as our friendship.

It's impossible to view hospitality as anything other than an extension of the social graces. They are so intangibly linked. The moral of this chapter is that when you entertain, you are really putting yourself on display. People take notice and appreciate how you handle yourself and others. Don't wait until the night before your first big dinner party to start boning up on your etiquette. Things will go tremendously smoother if you have an idea of what to expect or what to do should the unexpected show up one night at your door.

> *It is wise to apply the oil*
> *of refined politeness to the*
> *mechanism of friendship.*
>
> COLETTE

CHAPTER TWO

Basic Etiquette

"A CRASH COURSE IN MANNERS"

$\mathcal{G}$ood manners are not a thing of the past. They are alive and well in considerate and loving people. Armed with this chapter, you will not have to spend a lifetime cultivating proper poise and refinement. Consider this fast food etiquette. If you are only able to read one chapter of this book before your next dinner party or bridal luncheon, let it be this one. We have highlighted here the basics of etiquette to serve as your guide in most of the social situations in modern living.

THE DINNER PARTY

FASHIONABLY ON TIME

Being "fashionably late" is a thing of the past. Nowadays it is considered a huge faux pas and is incredibly inconsiderate to your hosts. The standard rule is no earlier than and no more than fifteen minutes late. The guest that arrives more than fifteen minutes after the function begins is being insensitive. Even if you are known to always be late, you are still not excused from this rule. Punctuality shows attention to detail and your interest in the social event. Hosts always appreciate being able to start entertaining their guests on time.

INTRODUCTIONS

You never get a second chance to make a first impression. Putting our best foot forward when meeting new

people is a goal we should all strive for. Socially, as your sphere of influence widens, new people will be added to your life. Do not hold back waiting to be introduced.

Introduce Younger People to Older People:

"Mother, may I introduce Scarlett O'Hara? Scarlett, I'd like you to meet my mother, Virginia Bell."

Introduce Men to Women:

"Scarlett, I'd like you to meet Rhett Butler. Rhett, this is my friend Scarlett O'Hara."

Introduce People to People in Authority:

"Mr. President, I'd like to introduce Melanie Wilkes."

Introducing Yourself:

When attending a party, you should not expect your host to introduce you to all of the guests. Take the initiative. Introduce yourself to a guest and offer your hand for a handshake.

Upon meeting a new acquaintance the following responses are appropriate:

- "Nice to meet you."
- "How are you?"
- "Hello."

> *When you see a person slip down on the ice, do not laugh at them... It is more feminine on witnessing such a sight, to utter an involuntary scream.*
> ELIZA LESLIE, *MISS LESLIE'S BEHAVIOR BOOK*

Friendly small talk will often accompany an introduction. Following are further guidelines regarding introductions.

Women

Today, women shake hands when they are introduced to a man or to a woman. They have the choice to sit or stand when introduced. With so many women working and using business courtesies, most favor standing when introduced.

Men

A man should always rise when he is introduced to a man or a woman and he should extend his hand for a handshake.

Children

Children should be taught to respect adults. They should stand up when an adult enters the room and shake hands when it is offered. Children should not call adults by their first names unless given permission to do so.

Awkward Moments

Have you ever had someone greet you with "I bet you don't remember me?" This is the epitome of an awkward moment. You should graciously say, "Momentarily, your name has slipped my mind." Don't get pulled into guessing who they are.

Handicapped

If you are introduced to a physically handicapped person it is best to let them take the lead. Certainly, a warm smile and a verbal greeting is enough for anyone.

THE HOSTESS GIFT

It is customary to bring a small gift with you when you are being entertained in a person's home for a meal or when staying overnight. This gift, known as a bread and butter gift, shows your appreciation for their kindness towards you. The gift usually consists of flowers, gourmet food, candy, wine, or some special treat. The gift should not be a dessert or something to be eaten with the meal.

When giving flowers, make sure that you don't cause your hostess to search for a container and fix the flowers. A pot of planted herbs makes a nice gift.

Although it is lovely to bring a gift, it is best not to overdo or underdo. An overly extravagant gift will make your hostess feel awkward and embarrassed. The same is true of underdoing the hostess gift. Imagine how awkward your hostess would feel receiving a bouquet of flowers a little past their bloom. Keep in mind that the gift need not be wrapped. Simply put it in a decorative bag. It is handed to the hostess as you are greeted at the door.

Good manners spring from just one thing—kind impulses.

ELSA MAXWELL, *ELSA MAXWELL'S ETIQUETTE BOOK*

YOUR ROLE AS A GUEST

When you have been invited to someone's home you are in a position of honor. Whether it is for a meal or for an overnight stay, you need to be considerate of the family and fit into their schedule.

Important Things for a Guest to Remember:

- Be punctual, but not early.
- Cancel only if there is an emergency.
- Make it a point to speak with the other guests.
- Offer to help the hostess.
- Wear appropriate attire—if you are unsure, ask the hostess.
- Do not go to the party ill.
- Don't be the last to leave.
- Always tell your hostess you enjoyed the evening when you leave.
- Call your hostess the next day to tell her you enjoyed the evening and write a thank-you note immediately.

THE OVERNIGHT STAY

HOW TO BE A GOOD HOUSEGUEST

Make sure your hosts know of your arrival time and notify them of any delays.

When you're an overnight houseguest, you should clean up after yourself. For example, take your used glass and place it in the dishwasher. Do not create more work for your hostess.

The gracious guest will observe the hosts' privacy and not snoop or open drawers that are private. This includes

helping yourself to anything in the refrigerator. If the hostess invites you to do so, you should still be modest about eating their food.

Remember that as a guest, you are to blend in with the family. You should be sensitive about not using all the hot water, listening to the television loudly, or asking for too many items that you forgot. Consider the bedtime hours of your hosts. If they are early-to-bed folks, simply go to your room and read quietly. It is always a good idea to bring reading material to entertain yourself.

Hang your wet towels on a hook (do not leave them balled up on the floor). Always, always make up your bed unless it's departure day. Keep your room tidy and, on the day you leave, take your sheets off the bed, fold them, and place them on the bed.

Rules for the Overnight House Guest

* Pick up after yourself.
* Make up your bed.
* Remove your personal items from the bathroom (unless it's private).
* Keep the bathroom clean.
* Never use the phone without permission.
* Treat the house and all things in it with your utmost respect.
* Make your schedule fit into your host's schedule.
* Always offer to help.
* Tell your hosts the exact time of your arrival and departure and honor these times.

YOUR ROLE AS A HOSTESS

A hostess has the responsibility of entertaining her guest or guests. Her most important duties are introducing the

guests to each other and keeping the tone of the evening on an even tempo. The best hostess is an organized hostess who can plan the meal, serve it, and entertain her guests.

Making your guests feel special and comfortable is the mark of a gracious host or hostess. Upon taking their coat, offer your guest liquid refreshment. It is nice to say, "I am offering Perrier or raspberry tea. Which may I get for you?" You should then serve them their drink with a napkin.

What to Do with House Guests?

It is a gracious hostess who allows her house guests to sleep in for as long as they wish, but this does not mean that the hostess should rearrange her plans for the sake of the guests' beauty rest. Also keep in mind the bathing schedules of your guests as well as your family's. If possible, it is always best to discuss your schedules prior to their visit.

Guest Safety

Not only do you need to see to your guests' comforts, it's also important to see to their safety. Fill them in on where the nearest exits are and what to do and who to call in case of an emergency. This will allow them to sleep better at night.

Unannounced Guests

The mark of a good host is the ability to deal with things as they come. This includes unexpected guests. Technically, you are under no obligation to offer lodgings or hospitality to those who just show up on your front door. Realistically, however, you may find it difficult and somewhat painful to turn away from a guest in need.

Be a Good Listener

Being a good listener is vital for good communication. Some of the most interesting people that you will ever meet are incredible listeners. An experienced hostess will usually place a talker next to a listener. This tends to balance the conversation at the dinner table.

THE BASICS OF DRESSING

Dressing appropriately is one of the sure signs of etiquette success. It is preferable to be understated than overstated anytime. Following is a helpful guide to the six main categories of basic dressing. If you follow this, be assured that you will never spend another embarrassing moment dressed in the wrong thing again.

*If a man be gracious and courteous
to strangers, it shows he is a citizen of
the world and that his heart is no island
cut off from other lands,
but a continent that joins to them.*

FRANCIS BACON

A Woman's Dress

Formal (White Tie)

This is often a full-skirted dress that is suitable for dancing. Its length should not quite reach the floor. She should also wear long, elbow-length gloves, shoes with heels, and jewelry.

Formal (Black Tie)

Either a cocktail dress, a dinner suit of street length, or a long, formal evening dress is appropriate for black tie affairs. Gloves may or may not be worn.

Semi-Formal

This attire includes a mid-length dress or gown, shoes, and possibly a shoulder wrap. The key to this category is to dress elegantly, yet also to remain comfortable.

Informal

A mid-length dress or pant suit can be worn in this category.

Business

Again, a mid-length dress or pant suit is acceptable. Suits with jackets are highlighted in this category. Dark shoes take the higher points.

Casual

This is the fun category for women. Where men are slightly restricted to what they may or may not wear, women are free in this category to make their own decisions (for the most part). Just remember to dress along the same lines as the other party goers.

A Man's Attire

The way a man dresses is no small matter. Knowing the basics is *very* important.

White Tie

White tie includes, quite obviously, a white tie, plus a wing collar, a tailcoat, black trousers and socks, and plain black shoes. Seldom is this type of dress requested nowadays, except for events at the White House, some weddings, debuts, and balls. When dressing, think of the Cary Grantish movie roles—debonair and very chic.

Black Tie

Black tie is one of the most formal dress types. An invitation may not always specify the kind of formal dress required. If that is the case, black tie is understood to be the appropriate choice. Black tie evening wear consists of the following:

- Black jacket (single or double breasted, depending on your preference).
- Black trousers (with a satin or grosgrain faille down the outside leg seam).
- Black shoes with black dress socks.
- White (front-pleated) dress shirt or tuxedo shirt.
- Waistcoat or cummerbund (never both).
- Bow tie (made of dressy silk or satin). Traditionally this is a black bow tie.

Semi-Formal

A white jacket, dark trousers, a bow tie, or a pleated or ruffled shirt, a cummerbund, and black shoes define the semi-formal approach. You may, if you so desire, select patterns or colors for the bow tie and cummerbund.

Business

This is a suit with a dress shirt, a full-length tie, dark socks, and black shoes.

Informal or Casual

Business attire also works for this or you can choose to dress in nice slacks, a sport jacket, dress shirt, dark socks, and dark shoes. A tie is optional, but still preferred in certain social circles.

An Important Note:

Formal attire, for men and women, is never worn before six o'clock in the evening. If the function begins in the afternoon, the host should provide a place where his or her guests may dress for the formal evening. Think of Scarlet O'Hara at Ashley Wilkes' Twelve Oaks right before the Yankees came. Needless to say, this is hardly standard practice anymore.

Oh, and One More Thing . . .

The ever-eternal debate over Memorial Day! The tradition of wearing white only after Memorial Day is still alive and well in many areas. This marks the beginning of the warm weather (if you're in the South, the sweltering heat). This color choice continues until Labor Day, at which point it becomes one of the most common and most easily spotted faux pas in American tradition. Still, customs shift in different parts of the country. Although *most* people are probably aware of this rule, in the South it is a rule of thumb and violation of it is grounds for social reprimanding by your aunt.

Before We Go Any Further . . .

A note on shoe color: There exist more types and colors of shoes than words today. The conservative choice is always best (black). It's the safest bet. Always wear black for formal dress.

And ladies . . . wherever you go, whatever you do, remember to sit with your knees together or legs crossed. Don't slouch. Sit up straight, shoulders back and head high.

And fellas . . . not so fast, come back here. You have more freedom in this category, but never allow one's legs to spread in public. We don't wish to have to say another word on this issue.

> *Etiquette—a fancy word for*
> *simple kindness.*
>
> ELSA MAXWELL, *ELSA MAXWELL'S ETIQUETTE BOOK*

CHAPTER THREE

Table Manners

"MINDING YOUR P'S AND Q'S"

One of the few constants in all of our lives is that we eat. Dinner, quite often, is the only meal where we can relax and take our time. But rushing to make it to work in the morning or running errands during your lunch hour doesn't mean you can relax your manners. Who knows where life will lead you? You may find yourself dining in the White House one evening.

Table etiquette, or the proper way of handling yourself during a meal, could mean the difference in your career. When I (Susan) worked as a recruiter, many of my clients included dinner as part of the interview. This allows the company to observe the person's etiquette. Good etiquette can do wonders to impress your interviewers and advance your candidacy for a position. On the other hand, bad etiquette can act just as quickly to dash your chances of getting a job as a bad interview.

By practicing correct etiquette at home, it will soon become a natural part of your lifestyle. You will think of basic table manners not as strict rules, but as natural extensions of yourself. More than anything else, good manners will put you at ease in a variety of social situations. Whether it be a small gathering of intimate friends or a large Christmas dinner, you will be more at ease and relaxed if you know which fork to use or when it is considered proper to begin eating. Being relaxed allows you

to sparkle in the social setting and to laugh and to enjoy the company of those who surround you as well as let them see the real you. It may seem trivial, but for anyone who has ever been in a strange situation it's nerve-racking. Stop the anxiety before it starts! Learn these simple rules and you'll find that you will dazzle everyone with your seemingly effortless elegance and sophistication.

The Silver Setting

Being comfortable at a formal seated dinner is the ultimate challenge for all of us. The silver is lined up on both sides of the plate like menacing soldiers, and the novice could find it very intimidating. Understanding the silver setting is really just using common sense. If your first course is a salad, then your salad fork is on the outside. These are established rules that are easy to follow. If you are still baffled, observe your hostess and follow her lead.

You begin with the outside utensils and work your way in on both sides. The most formal dinners today are usually no more than four or five courses.

A. Napkin

B. Service plate

C. Soup bowl on a liner plate

D. Bread and butter plate with butter knife

E. Water glass

F. Red wine glass

G. White wine glass

H. Fish fork

I. Dinner fork

J. Salad fork

K. Dessert fork

L. Knife

M. Fish knife

N. Teaspoon

O. Soup spoon

FORMAL DINNER

A. Napkin

B. Luncheon plate

C. Soup (or other first course plate) on a liner plate

D. Bread and butter plate with butter knife

E. Water glass

F. Wine glass

G. Luncheon fork

H. Knife

I. Teaspoon

J. Soup spoon

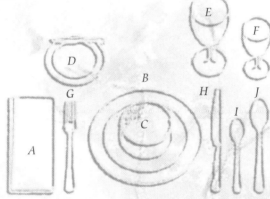

LUNCHEON

> There is no place in the world where courtesy is so necessary as in the home.
>
> HELEN HATHAWAY, *MANNERS*

LINENS

To set a beautiful table is one of the delights of a hostess. Gleaming crystal, china, and silver welcome the guest with warmth and graciousness. To correctly set the most formal table you would use your finest damask table-cloth and napkins.

For informal dining other tablecloths, place mats, and napkins are called for. This is when you are able to use your creative and imaginative talents to decorate. Coordinating linens with china has become a huge table top industry.

Recommendations for Table Linens:

- 1 Large, Formal Damask Tablecloth
- 12 Formal Damask Napkins
- 1 Liner for Above Tablecloth
- 1 Casual Tablecloth
- 8 Casual Napkins
- 1 Set of 8 Placemats and 8 Napkins (Dressy)
- 1 Set of 8 Placemats and 8 Napkins (Casual)

GUIDE TO TABLE SETTINGS

BUFFET

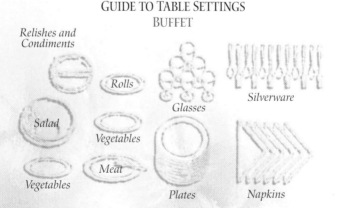

Relishes and Condiments

Rolls

Glasses

Silverware

Salad

Vegetables

Vegetables

Meat

Plates

Napkins

Resting Position

Finished Position

> *Much of good manners is about knowing when to pretend that what's happening isn't happening.*
> MRS. FALK FEELEY

SEATING

Traditionally, seat your guests male, female, male, female. In addition to this, the man sits to the left of the woman he has escorted to the dinner party. The following is an example of dinner-guest seating:

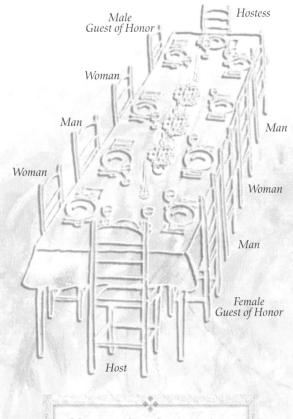

Male
Guest of Honor

Hostess

Woman

Man

Man

Woman

Woman

Man

Female
Guest of Honor

Host

> Manners and morals are twin shoots
> from the same root.
>
> AGNES H. MORTON, *ETIQUETTE*

The host and hostess of the dinner party sit at either end of the table, opposite of each other.

If the dinner is being held in honor of a particular person or persons, these honored guests are seated close to the ends of the table, near the host or hostess. They are never seated in the middle of the table.

THE STAFF

If you will need to hire attendants to assist you with your dinner party, you may make arrangements with a professional catering service. For more informal and smaller gatherings you may find sufficient help from temporary hiring agencies. You may also want to contact a local restaurant or hotel to see if any of their employees will work on the weekends or during their off hours. Or another possibility is to ask a good friend to help you serve and assist in the clearing and cleaning of the dishes.

THE MENU

For larger gatherings, it is probably best to work with a catering service. These professional services make it their business to keep track of the tiniest details to ensure that your dinner party goes off without a hitch. The catering company will estimate how much food you will need to take care of the needs of your guests.

Although having your function professionally catered will remove a lot of the guesswork from planning the menu, a good hostess will keep track of the food and drink consumption and be prepared with extra food and drink to prevent the kitchen from running out before the party ends.

If you are preparing a formal dinner yourself, courses should be planned as follows:

First Course—The Appetizer

This can be nuts, canapés, or anything on a tray passed in the living room before being seated for dinner.

Second Course—Soup or Fish

Usually this is a light course.

Third Course—Salad

When serving salad with all the other courses, keep it simple. Crisp greens and a tasty vinaigrette dressing are always a wonderful treat.

Fourth Course—Entree

This is of course the main course. It usually consists of meat or fish with vegetables and a starch.

Fifth Course—Dessert and Coffee

Dessert can be fruit and cheese or cake. The French serve a chocolate and a vanilla or cream dessert.

TABLE MANNERS FOR US ALL

The hostess is the person to observe and take your cues from. Wait for the hostess to be seated before you take a seat. The gentleman always seats the lady to his right. He pulls out her chair for her and once she is seated he then takes his seat beside her.

THE NAPKIN

Once again you take your cue from your hostess. She may place her napkin in her lap before the blessing or wait until after to do so.

- You may unfold your napkin, but leave it folded in half with the fold against your body.
- If you leave the table during the meal, place your napkin on your chair seat.
- At the end of the meal, place your napkin to the right of your plate. It does not need to be folded.

THE ABSOLUTE TABLE MANNERS DO'S

- Always sit according to the instructions of your hostess.
- Taste your food before adding extra salt or pepper.
- Close your mouth while chewing.
- Be careful not to make noise with your silverware.
- Match your eating pace with that of the other guests—not too slow and not too fast.
- Sit up straight in your chair.
- Say only good things about the food. If you can't, then say nothing at all.
- Always be gracious with your words and actions.
- Always show your appreciation for the efforts of others.
- Be polite and patient with the other guests.
- Watch your hostess for important cues.
- Most importantly, enjoy yourself!

Wrong, wrong, wrong
Will never be right, right, right!
ANN PLATZ

CHAPTER FOUR

Money Manners

"DON'T LEAVE HOME WITHOUT 'EM!"

*H*andling money is a very sensitive issue at home and in public. Whether you have a lot of money or barely any, it is always a touchy issue. I (Ann) can add that the misunderstanding of money in a foreign country is most definitely a cause for exasperation. My husband and I were vacationing in Rome, Italy. One night we dined at a lovely Italian restaurant near the Spanish steps. During the meal, a strolling violinist played for each guest. At the end of the music, my husband reached for a tip and gave the maestro four huge, impressive coins that were silver and gold. The maestro threw his nose up in the air and stomped off in protest. Later we found out that my husband had given him less than ten cents. That was our first night in Rome.

THE FINE ART OF TIPPING

Tipping is the way we thank people for providing a service for us. The amount of the tip should equal your satisfaction with the services rendered. The average tip, or gratuity, is between fifteen and twenty percent before taxes. Naturally, if you have dined for hours and the service has been exceptional, you should tip at least twenty percent. If, however, you feel the service you received was less

than satisfactory, you should ask to speak to the manager. Do this especially if you experience rudeness.

Restaurant Tipping

If you are in a very fine restaurant, you should tip the coat check person one or two dollars. The person who walks you to the table is called the host and does not require a tip. In the rest rooms, you should tip the attendant between fifty cents and a dollar. There is usually a dish there to place your tip.

If you frequent a restaurant often, you can slip a five to twenty dollar tip to the host once in a while. If the restaurant arranges for live music, you may tip the musician one dollar. The tip for valet parking is from one to two dollars upon the delivery of your car. If you are having an affair catered, you should tip the servers fifteen percent.

Cafeterias and Buffets

No tip is required at a cafeteria- or buffet-style service restaurant. Only tip if a service person brings you a beverage. The tip would be around ten percent and is left on the table.

Beauty Salons, Flower Shops, Etc.

With services provided at businesses like beauty salons or flower shops, tipping the boss is optional. But other employees should receive the following:

- Hairdressers or barbers 15-20%
- Manicurists $2.00
- Shampooist $2.00

Airport Tipping

The uniformed people that meet you at curbside to assist you with your luggage are called skycaps. Tips are a large part of their salaries. You should tip one dollar per bag for their service.

Services, Etc.

Service providers such as doormen, the paper boy, UPS, and Fed Ex delivery people need not be tipped, but it is nice to recognize them at Christmas with either a gift of money (twenty dollars) or a present. Remember, it is nice to feel appreciated.

HOW TO PAY THE PIPER

Money usually complicates matters. And trying to pay the bill at a restaurant can be exceptionally complicated. Following is a story of two friends who were on the verge of really cementing their relationship. Money could have posed a problem, yet they chose not to let it negatively affect them.

Soon after Forrest began dating Kathleen, he invited her to have dinner with him at an elegant restaurant in Atlanta. He and Kathleen were beginning to fall in love with each other. Forrest wanted everything to be perfect.

The evening was wonderful. They enjoyed the food and the conversation. After dinner, Forrest pulled out his new corporate credit card and handed it to the waiter.

After a few minutes, the waiter returned and asked to speak privately with Forrest. The waiter explained that the credit card company had asked him to return Forrest's credit card to them. It had been rejected. Flabbergasted, Forrest asked why. The waiter didn't have an answer for him, but he did not return the card to Forrest.

When he came back to the table, Forrest sheepishly laughed. "He took my credit card," he said as he scratched his head. "This has to be a mistake." Forrest was a prominent CEO of a large corporation and he couldn't possibly see why his new company card would be rejected. He hadn't even used it yet.

Forrest laughs today and says that Kathleen married him knowing that her credit card could be retrieved at any place and at any moment! As this story illustrates, how you choose to handle a situation will define you as a person with or without great social grace. Be like Forrest.

Paying the Bill

Paying the bill at a restaurant can be awkward when you have not planned ahead. If you have invited the guest, then it is your party and you should expect to pay the bill.

Whatever you do, don't fight over the bill in the restaurant. Kindly tell the waiter ahead of time that you are the host and that you will be taking care of the check.

Sharing the Wealth

If everyone is to be responsible for their share of the bill, then make sure this is understood at the beginning. It is perfectly fine to go "Dutch treat." You can ask for separate checks at the start of the meal and that makes everything easy.

Great persons are able to do
great kindnesses.

MIQUEL DE CERVANTES

CHAPTER FIVE

Business Etiquette

"CORPORATE COURTESIES"

$\mathscr{E}$veryone has dreams of climbing the ladder of corporate success. Just as we pointed out in the chapter on Table Manners, the social and the business arenas often intersect. To move up in one, you have to be able to move up in the other. Whether it is a breakfast, lunch, or dinner meeting, business people should use this opportunity to capitalize on their personal etiquette.

THE CORPORATE DINING EXPERIENCE

The place where proper etiquette really shows up is while you are eating dinner with someone. Most large corporations consider the dining experience the last part of the interview process for the potential executive. After all, your interviewers want to see if you can handle yourself socially, since business quite often involves fancy socializing. If you do not value, nor appreciate, the simple rules that define social norms and values, then what will others who appreciate these rules think of you? It's about finding common ground. You can always count on social graces to achieve this.

The Corporate "Dinner Date"

One of the first rules of dining is that the person who does the inviting also does the hosting. Therefore it is customary for them to pick up the tab. If the business meeting is among people from the office and is an "official meeting," then the company pays for it and the one who called the meeting handles paying the bill.

HOSTING A BUSINESS MEETING

Conducting a business meeting in the proper way is very important to the business-savvy person. In today's busy world, many business-related events happen after business hours. At these events, the guests will once again take their cues from the host, who sets the tone for the evening. For instance, the host usually seats the guest where he or she needs to be. Also, the host will often help with suggestions of what to order. Most people order one or two courses and usually stay in the middle of the price range. It is clearly out of place to order the most expensive item on the menu.

The host will lead the conversation and usually not discuss business until after the meal. Then everyone is free to discuss business. These after-hours meetings can be more valuable than you realize. It gives one a chance to interact with business associates on a social level rather than strictly during office hours.

The host should never assume that everyone knows each other. He should introduce each guest to the entire group. It is extremely unacceptable for the host to spend all of his or her time speaking to only one person.

As the host of the meeting, he or she is also responsible for preparing and typing an agenda, having coffee and iced water available, and providing a pad and pen for each guest. It is also very important to stay in the preset time frame of the meeting and to make sure to discuss all relevant points.

The host should also make arrangements to have all of his or her telephone calls held till after the meeting. Being thoughtful in business meetings is a courtesy that others appreciate. After all, the people attending the meeting are giving up their time for this discussion. They deserve respect and consideration as well as appreciation.

It is the duty of the host to both begin and end the business meeting. When you are the host, it is also your responsibility to ensure that nothing occurs at the business meeting that should not occur at the office. Your good manners and social graces will long be remembered both as a positive reflection of you and as a positive reflection on the company that hired you.

LYING, BUSINESS STYLE

Lying is lying is lying is lying. Lying has no place in the workplace. Lying can take many forms and this includes making empty promises or telling people what they want to hear, regardless of what the truth is. "Let's do lunch," "The check is in the mail," "Oh, I was just thinking of you," and "I was up all night going over your proposal" are examples of lying, business style. Remember, if you want others to respect you and to trust you, you have to demonstrate that you are a person who deserves trust and respect.

HOW TO SEVER A BUSINESS RELATIONSHIP

As important as business contacts and relationships are, it sometimes becomes necessary to sever a relationship. This requires a delicate combination of wisdom and tact, and calls upon all of your social graces and patience. If you can end these relationships graciously and tactfully, you will save some of the efforts that you have made.

One example might be: "I believe that we have come to a good stopping point."

SIMPLE BUSINESS ETIQUETTE

The Greeting

When greeting a guest of your company's, both men and women should stand. This is a courtesy and a show of respect. Next, offer your hand for a firm handshake. After inviting them to have a seat you should offer a beverage. Never make your guest or visitor wait more than a few minutes. Respect their time as they do yours. You should do everything within your power to make them feel welcomed and special. This is usually the first impression that they have of your company. As they say, first impressions are important. Make them count.

Phone Manners

In today's global economy, often the company's first contact and interaction with a potential business associate, partner, or client takes place over the telephone. Good telephone manners are a must. You take responsibility for sending your company's image and reputation over the telephone line. If you are going to reach out and touch someone, it is better to leave them with a positive impression.

The Importance of Being Prompt

Being prompt and efficient in all areas is a must in the business world. Not only is it good etiquette, it's also good business. Being on time says a lot about your relationship with your client. However, if you find that you are going to be more than five minutes late, call ahead to let the person know.

Being prompt applies to phone calls as well. Returning a telephone call in a prompt fashion is a must in a mannerly world. Use an answering machine if you have to, for it is better to leave a message than to keep missing the person you are calling. If you are leaving a message for someone to return your telephone call, always leave your full name and telephone number. Don't assume that they can remember your phone number. In returning a call, if you have left two messages and have still not received a call back, you are no longer obligated to continue to call.

Personal Telephone Calls

Personal telephone calls are usually frowned upon at work. Yet sometimes they become unavoidable and you must make a personal call or handle some personal business during your normal business hours. If this comes about, make sure to limit these to your lunch hour or morning break. Try not to mix your business and your personal life. This demonstrates your commitment to your professional image and career.

Business Thank-You Notes

Another important must in the business world is the all-important thank-you note. This note should be handwritten and should express your gratitude for time offered and services rendered. Write thank-you notes for gifts that are given to you within the week that the gift is given. Always write business letters on business stationery. Although faxes and e-mail have brought business correspondence to new levels, it is never appropriate to fax or e-mail a thank-you note.

Business Cards

Business cards are a good way to both promote your own career as well as the livelihood of your company. You should have a card with the name of your business, address, telephone numbers, and fax number printed on it. It is important that your business card reflects the personality of your business.

THE IMPORTANCE OF RESPECT WITHIN THE OFFICE

We have already spoken on the crucial role that respect plays in the business world. Respect demonstrates your professional commitment to clients and business peers. It is also important to extend this same respect to those working in the same company as you do. Respect the privacy and the boundaries of your co-workers. Do not read their mail or office memos. Do not give unsolicited opinions. They will ask for your advice if and when they need it. Make sure to always knock on someone's office door before entering. Then ask them if it is a convenient time to talk with them. Be considerate. Return things that you borrow. There is nothing more aggravating than to desperately search for something that has not been returned only to realize it hours later. Show kindness and consideration of your co-workers by doing the following things:

- Refrain from smoking in the office.
- Clean up after yourself in the break room.
- Wait for your turn in the conversation.
- Support your fellow workers.
- Look for the best in your peers.
- Be courteous.
- Respect others' faith or religion.
- Consider others' privacy.

- Be a team player.
- Be on time.
- Finish your work on time.
- Keep your work space tidy. Treat it as you would treat your home.

Your Assistant Is Your Helper

You've had a hard day. The boss didn't like your proposal. Your kids are sick at home. The dog needs to be picked up at the vet and you still haven't done your grocery shopping. Life is tough and juggling business with the personal along with your ego is difficult. It's understandable that you are under a lot of stress, but so are those who are trying to help you.

A happy work environment is one in which there is mutual respect and consideration for each other. Restrain your temper before it blows up in your face. You'll feel better and your assistant will be much happier. Working well together will make the two of you an unstoppable team.

OFFICE DRESS

Another important factor is appropriate office attire. Do not overdress or underdress in the office. "Conservative" is the word here. For women, low-cut blouses, short skirts, and revealing dresses are definitely out. Unless there are clear cut rules in the office, always take your cues from what others are wearing. These days, more and more companies are having Friday as casual day in the office. Again, the key here is not to over or underdress. You must strike a balance. Casual office dress is an effort to relax the office coat-and-tie atmosphere before the weekend. This is a gift, not a given. Dress appropriately and professionally.

When attending office parties or occasions that involve out-of-office entertaining, it is safer to stay more to the conservative side of dress unless otherwise stated. This is not the same dress as for a personal social function. Stay with conservative-cut clothing and conservative colors.

OFFICE ROMANCE

Since the introduction of women in the work force, businesses have had to deal with the issues of office romances. The practice of office romances used to be frowned upon and, in many cases, became cause for dismissal from the company. Today, this rule is not as strict. And with the emphasis so strongly placed on careers, men and women often find their spouses as they date, fall in love, and marry their co workers.

Most employers are interested in their employees concentrating on their work and not on their co-workers. An office romance can, and often does, lead to distraction. So, if you become interested in a fellow worker, try to be as discreet as possible. Don't take advantage of situations that could possibly generate office gossip. If you choose to date a fellow worker and the relationship ends, you might feel awkward around them in the day-to-day workplace. If the breakup does indeed become painful, you may find yourself looking for another job.

PRAYER IN THE OFFICE

Although you might do a lot of praying in the hope of finishing a project on time, limit this to yourself unless you have a clear understanding with your co-workers. Prayer is a very private matter and everyone seems to have a different opinion of it and its place. Some companies may even sponsor voluntary prayer groups, but these only work if the employees feel no corporate pressure to attend.

OFFICE PARTIES

Of course, you always have the option to regretfully inform your boss that you will be unable to attend his barbecue next weekend, but you may feel the pressure to do so anyway. Office politics being what they are, it's often the person who is most visible, both during and after hours, who gets the promotion. This visibility demonstrates that, no matter the time, no matter the day, you're available for the company. There are definitely pros and cons with office parties, so be sure to make up your own mind about them. Your behavior should be impeccable. A good idea is to plan to attend the function for a short period. This way, you have the option to leave or stay. By doing this, you won't feel manipulated or trapped.

IT'S POSSIBLE TO BE FRIENDS

The overall rule in business etiquette and corporate courtesies is to carve out a niche for yourself while simultaneously working within the structure of the company. It is definitely important to retain your individualism, yet you must remember that the moment you enter the office workplace you are part of a diverse and skilled team. The same social graces that apply to general life also apply here. Be conscientious and respectful of others. Be kind and loving and sincere. Do these things and you will find that your life, both personally and professionally, will be blessed beyond words.

Where there is love,
there are manners.

SUSAN WALES

CHAPTER SIX

The Art of Conversation

"FROM CHIT-CHAT TO STORYTELLING"

Conversation is an art form.

The spoken word is our best form of communication. With words we can touch other people and help them to see the world from our vantage point, if only for a few minutes. We can use words to make others laugh, smile, cry, think, share. Every human emotion, every thought, has a word for it. We just have to decide how we want to use these words.

Listening to a person who possesses the gift of conversation is delightful. Some people are natural talkers. They are very much at ease communicating with others. These "naturals" are easy to spot. People gravitate to them at parties or in a crowded hall somewhere. People love to speak with the naturals because during the entire conversation they feel like equal and valued partners. A good conversationalist makes others feel special and listened to. They radiate love, joy, and emotion.

Both of my parents (Ann's) were fabulous storytellers and "held court" when they told their tales. My parents were naturals. Some people have it and others don't, but please don't despair. You can be a fine conversationalist without "the gift." In many ways, being a listener is even better than being a talker. So many people want to talk and entertain, while only a handful are content to listen and smile.

My (Susan's) husband, Ken Wales, is a charismatic conversationalist and speaker from whom we can learn invaluable lessons. Ken is never introduced without looking directly into the person's eyes and asking, "Tell me what interests you?" He makes a special effort to draw the attention away from himself directly onto the individual with whom he is speaking.

Ken has a charming way of drawing a group into the topic by inviting the audience to participate. He always ends his speeches with a question and answer session. It's easy to understand how Ken makes others feel so special.

Learning how to feel comfortable in a group will require being an active part of the conversation. As in all other areas of etiquette, the art of conversation requires balance. It's about giving and receiving, about thinking and reacting, about listening and perceiving. You must strike a balance between your participation and whomever else is involved in the discussion. Think about all those awkward moments you've undoubtedly spent listening to someone go on and on about his three dogs and vacations in Aspen for the last fifteen years. Others are not interested in everything about your life. So don't dominate the conversation, but bring others into it. People love to feel involved and welcomed to be involved.

TO LISTEN IS DIVINE

A good conversationalist is one that begins with a considerate heart and who is genuinely interested in the person that they are speaking with. Being a good listener is one of the most important skills you will ever learn. Listening affects every facet of your life, from important business matters to what time you are meeting your mother for dinner. Everyone wants to be heard. Listening is a form of great respect.

TABLE TALK

Good table conversation separates an average party from one that is special and memorable. In a large gathering it is polite to talk to the other guests. Establishing eye contact with the person you are speaking with is necessary. Eye contact speaks of self-confidence and interest in whom you're talking to. A good hostess knows how to get her guests talking and also how to move the conversation around the table to include each guest. The hostess usually keeps the tempo going by introducing new topics and by simply asking the guests a question. General topics are the order of the day.

Examples of Successful Topics:

- "Don't grandchildren say the cutest things?"
- "I hear we're due for some fabulous weather this fall."
- "Have you been to the new restaurant on the corner of Main and Smith Street?"

As different as we are on the outside, our external differences pale in comparison with our individual thoughts and beliefs. No matter how skilled the hostess, there are just some subjects that should be omitted from the conversation altogether. Examples of these taboo subjects are the issue of the death penalty, abortion, details of an operation, or topics that are just too intimate for discussion in the dining room. This is an area where common sense should rule.

If you are still nervous about making interesting table talk, prepare yourself before an outing. Become well-informed by reading newspapers, being current in global news, and by simply doing your homework about the interests and hobbies of the people you will be with. It is always charming when someone knows a little about you.

SMALL TALK OR WHAT WE CALL IN THE SOUTH, "CHIT-CHAT"

Small talk is what is required when you are meeting someone for the first time. Basic etiquette calls for eye contact and a firm handshake. Small talk can sometimes be a nerve-racking experience, especially if you cannot think of anything to say. It is always a good idea to start the conversation by asking the person about themselves. This way, you not only endear yourself, but you also generate a subject to discuss. It is best to avoid getting too personal. Instead, stay general in your conversation. For example: "Mary tells me that you grow the most beautiful roses."

A WORD TO THE WISE . . .

Respecting the other person's right to their own view-point is not only mannerly . . . it's refreshing. Intense conversations should be reserved for courtrooms, debates, and negotiations. Definitely not for social situations! No matter where you are, there are a few topics that have always been, and will always be, taboo when it comes to topics open for discussion.

- Salary or net worth
- Commissions
- Promotions
- Job searches

- Your sex life
- Somebody else's sex life
- Someone's sexual orientation
- Age
- Affairs
- Criminal activities
- Weight

"DID YOU HEAR THE ONE ABOUT THE . . . ?"

Joking makes us seem witty and worldly. Everyone wants to be the person with the great sense of humor and a way with words. We want people to like us and to be drawn to our magnetic personalities. This is good. But joking can also be destructive.

A practical joke draws its humor from belittling another person or persons. It encourages others to make fun of someone at their expense. Be creative and find other ways to be the life of the party.

> *Without good manners,*
> *you'll fall off the ladder of success.*
> SUSAN WALES

RUDE AND OFFENSIVE COMMENTS

Usually rude and offensive people do not know that they are rude and offensive. They do not think about what they say or how it will affect the person they are speaking with. Regardless if they intend to be rude and offensive or not, every now and then someone will say something out of place. Instead of correcting them it is better to ignore it and change the subject.

Vulgar language or obscene remarks are always, let us repeat that, *always* out of place in conversation. Even if you think the person you are speaking with is all right with the language, don't use it. It simply does not have a place. If you chose to incorporate these words into your daily vocabulary, please be mindful of others. Especially in venues like restaurants and other public places, be careful and considerate of others. If someone near you in a restaurant or stadium uses such language on a regular basis, it is perfectly acceptable for you to ask them to stop. "Would you mind not using such language, please?" There is no guaranteed response, however. They may realize what they sound like and stop or they may continue. Either way you demonstrate your disapproval.

I'M REALLY, TRULY SORRY

Apologizing is an important skill to learn, since it seems to come up almost daily and for some of us, hourly. Apologizing is important because it is our best response when we do something wrong. A verbal or written apology can soothe and restore a bruised relationship. Good etiquette and good morals dictate that we should accept our wrongdoing as eagerly as we accept the things we do right. It is a very gracious person who can do both.

INAPPROPRIATE PLACES FOR CONVERSATIONS

Even though intense conversations may start up anywhere from coffee shops to bookstores, there are just some places where it is inappropriate to engage in lengthy discussion. The list that follows highlights some of the most common places where people want to be left alone to handle their business and their own thoughts.

- Libraries
- Rest rooms
- Religious services
- Funerals
- Theaters
- Museums
- Waiting rooms
- Elevators
- Newsstands
- Airplanes
- Buses, taxis, etc.
- Restaurants
- Supermarkets

Although in the above places it is normally best to mind your own business, one should still never forget the niceties of casual contact. For example, you should make it a point to smile and acknowledge the presence of another person sharing the same space as you.

However, like everything else in life, there exist certain exceptions from the rules. Airplane travel is one of them. Often passengers find themselves chatting with the person seated next to them. It's a fairly common experience because, after all, we're social creatures. Sometimes by the end of the flight you feel as if you've made a new friend. Other times, you just want to read the new book you bought or take a cat nap before you arrive at your destination. It all depends on the circumstances.

The important thing to remember is that you should never be impolite to someone you meet casually. Yet, you should also be aware of what makes you comfortable and where your boundaries lie. Nowhere is it written that you need to follow the lead of someone else merely for the sake of being polite.

TO INTERRUPT OR NOT TO . . . THAT IS THE PROBLEM

So you've gotten as far as the actual conversation. People are talking, having a good time, laughing. Smile. Relax. You're doing just fine. Suddenly, there's a problem. What happens when there's an interruption? How do you handle that?

You can look at interruptions several different ways. First, you may be embroiled in a lovely conversation or an important business discussion when someone bungles in and interrupts the entire moment you were just having. So what do you do? How do handle such impoliteness?

Well, most people . . . let me rephrase that . . . most polite people will not interrupt another person's conversation unless it is truly important. Listening is an act of courtesy. If you are interrupted, you could say, "I'll be with you in a moment." This is a polite way to keep control of the conversation, which makes you feel good. The interrupter may be bringing important news like there is a fire in the building or that your car is being towed. But regardless of the news, it is still important for you to act in kindness and politeness.

If on the other hand, it becomes necessary for you to interrupt the conversations of others, you might say the tried and true, "Excuse me." Then wait patiently to be recognized. It doesn't matter what end you're coming from. The bottom line is be patient and polite and others should follow suit.

CORRECTING GRAMMAR

It is extremely improper to correct another person's grammar when they are talking with you. It is not acceptable unless it is your child, and then do it discreetly.

BORING CONVERSATIONS OR THE BRAGGART

We have all had to endure the self-centered person who assumes control over the conversation. If you are standing with a group of people caught in that situation, simply excuse yourself and walk away. If, however, you are seated at dinner and cannot graciously excuse yourself, it is up to the hostess to rescue her guest. Of course, this should be done in a charming way. If you have to deal with it on your own, you might say "That's an interesting viewpoint." Then turn to the guest on your other side and start a new conversation.

HOW TO END A CONVERSATION

Some people simply do not know how to end a conversation. It is as easy as "I sure have enjoyed talking with you." If it is a telephone conversation, the person calling is the one in charge of ending the conversation. Some examples in either situation would be:

- "Excuse me, I see someone I need to speak with."
- "Have you met the Smiths yet? Come with me. I'd like to introduce you."
- "It's been nice talking with you. I've enjoyed it."

COMPLIMENTS

An honest compliment is a refreshing gift to anyone. When offered to your hostess it is a lovely way of showing your gratitude for her efforts to entertain you. On the other hand, an exaggerated compliment is insincere and should be avoided. Always make sure to thank your hostess at the end of the meal. You could say:

- "What a lovely meal. You served some of my favorite dishes."
- "Thank you for including me in your lovely dinner party."

AND OH . . . THE BLESSINGS AND CURSES OF THE PHONE!

Once you've mastered the art of conversation with the people around you at work and at play, there is still another arena of confrontation which can possibly be the most hazardous of all: The Telephone.

The telephone is a marvelous invention. It provides us with almost unlimited access to the worlds of others. It connects us and allows us to "reach out and touch others." But this technology also allows others to reach out and touch you. This can be a good thing when your best friend calls about lunch next week or a bad thing when you're forced to deal with a pushy I'm-not-going-to-take-no-for-an-answer salesman.

Take heed. Arm yourself. Firmly repeat the following:

- "Thank you, but I don't do business over the telephone."
- "I don't take these types of calls at home."

WRONG NUMBERS

So there are a lot of numbers on that keypad and maybe you remember six out of the seven digits, and oh, you're not too sure if it was 404 or 440 for the area code. Whatever the reasons, there are a lot of them for making and receiving calls that are wrong numbers. It's how you deal with them that counts.

There is "the hang up." This is a disastrous wrong number solution. You hang up first, you feel guilty and, let's face it, basically a coward. Alternatively, someone hangs up on you and you get miffed and maybe even a bit paranoid. Was that Mother checking on me? Wrong. Wrong. Wrong. Bad. Bad. Bad. Is this sinking in?

Apply here what we already talked about, the art of apologizing. Apologize. Excuse yourself. Say something to the effect of, "Excuse me, I must have dialed the wrong number." If unsure about the number you just dialed, you can even tell the person at the other end the telephone number you thought you dialed. They will usually tell you if the number is correct. See all the useful information you gain by not hanging up?

If you still choose to handle the situation with the ill-fated hang-up call, be aware that many people have no problem with confronting their mis-caller. With the advent of Caller I.D. and * 69, they can find out who just rudely hung up on them. They may even call you back. Be warned.

WHAT TO DO IF THE PHONE RINGS?

All of our lives, we are conditioned that when the phone rings we pick it up. This is the Pavlovian bell and our triggered response is to pick up the phone. This, however, may not apply if you are at someone's home. Answer the phone only if your host asks you to first.

THE DO'S FOR A GOOD CONVERSATION:

- Share the conversation. Let everyone take a turn.
- Keep the talk interesting and light.
- Never embarrass your hostess.
- Never ask what something costs.
- Never use rude or shocking language.
- Keep personal problems private, especially at another person's expense.
- Be sincere with your compliments.
- Correct your spouse's etiquette, grammar, or behavior in private.
- Talk with the people on your left and right when dining.
- Be honest.
- Listen carefully.
- Be respectful.
- Learn to compromise.

> *Let no evil talk come out of your mouths,*
> *but only such as is good for edifying,*
> *as fits the occasion, that it may impart*
> *grace to those who hear.*
>
> THE BOOK OF EPHESIANS

CHAPTER SEVEN

Food Guide

"FOODS WE LOVE, BUT HAVE NO IDEA HOW TO EAT!"

*H*ow many times have you stared at a food and had absolutely no idea how to eat it? Whether you're willing to admit it or not, we have all had that experience at one time or another. I (Ann) remember my first artichoke. I chewed and chewed and chewed that leaf. I was so relieved when I saw another person simply pull the leaf through their teeth. From time to time, we all need someone to show us the way.

Below is a list of the "most difficult" foods to deal with. Some foods can be either finger foods or eaten with a fork. When in doubt, always use a fork. Study hard. Some foods were simply created to be difficult. It's like it's their mission. But if we go into our meals prepared, then we can be confident that we will triumph once and for all.

APPLES

When the apples are cut and in a salad, eat with a fork. If the apples are whole, cut the apple into quarters using a knife and fork. After that, the apple becomes a finger food.

ARTICHOKES

Artichokes are a finger food. They should be cooked until tender. Pull off one leaf at a time and dip into the sauce. Then pull through your teeth to scrape off the fleshy part of the artichoke. Place the remainder of the leaf on the side of your plate.

ASPARAGUS

You may eat asparagus with your fingers or with a knife and fork. Be sure not to overcook the asparagus so that they remain crisp and easy to pick up.

AVOCADOS

Avocados are usually served in dips or in salads and eaten with a fork. When they are served in halves, they are eaten with a spoon.

BACON

Bacon can be eaten with your fingers or a fork.

BANANAS

Bananas are eaten with the fingers when peeled and the peeling is placed on the plate. When cut up in a dish, they are eaten with a fork.

BARBECUED FOODS

If it is cooked on the grill, it can be eaten with your hands.

BERRIES

Eat berries using a spoon. Eat strawberries with your fingers.

BOUILLABAISSE

Bouillabaisse is a dish that includes fish and other seafood in a liquid base. It can be eaten with soup spoons, fish or regular knives, and shellfish crackers.

CAVIAR AND OTHER SPREADS

Caviar has long been regarded affectionately as the food of kings. It is a very expensive luxury food. It is spread on toast triangles with the use of a spreader and is eaten with your fingers. It may be garnished with hard boiled eggs, chopped onion, capers or lemon wedges. Any other spread you are confronted with will basically be the same, although not as expensive.

CLAMS ON THE HALFSHELL

Eat with a fish fork or salad fork. Do not eat the shells!

CLAMS OR OYSTERS, STEAMED

Have at it! Use your fingers!

CORN ON THE COB

Eat with both hands! Remember, corn handles can be inserted in each end.

DESSERTS

If it is bite-sized, eat your dessert with your fingers. Cakes and pies, however, should be eaten with a dessert spoon or fork.

FRIED CHICKEN

Ahh . . . one of the South's specialties and a personal favorite of ours. But whatever is the proper way to eat such a scary food? Don't sweat it. Enjoy the food, not the anxiety. When you're on a picnic, eat fried chicken with your fingers. When you're at the table, use a knife and fork. Don't worry, it still tastes the same.

FROG LEGS

Similar to fried chicken, frog legs can be eaten with the fingers, but a knife and fork are often preferred.

GRAPEFRUIT

Grapefruit should be served sectioned and easy to eat with a grapefruit spoon.

LEMONS AND LIMES

Whether you are served lemon slices, quarters, or halves, these are all considered acceptable finger foods.

LOBSTER

Crack lobster with a mallet. Pull the meat out with a seafood fork.

MELONS

When melons are served already cut up, then eat with a knife and fork. If the melons are served either cut in half or in wedges, eat using a spoon.

NUTS AND AFTER DINNER MINTS

At the most formal dinners, bowls of nuts will be on the table. Scoop nuts with a spoon and then eat with your fingers. If you are served an after-dinner mint simply take one at a time. Remember patience is a virtue.

OLIVES, CARROTS, CELERY, AND PICKLES

All of these may be eaten with the fingers.

PASTA

Pasta is one of the trickier foods, yet it remains one of the most popular with diners. Pasta should be eaten with a fork and a spoon that are used to twirl the pasta. If you prefer, you may cut it up and eat it with a fork.

> *Blessed are those who can give*
> *without remembering and take*
> *without forgetting.*
>
> ELIZABETH BIBESCO

PEAS

Peas should be eaten with a fork, not a spoon. You may use your knife to gather the peas onto your fork.

PIZZA

Eat pizza with your fingers or cut it up with a knife and fork.

POTATOES

French fries remain the ultimate finger food. But, if you prefer, it's perfectly acceptable to use a fork.

SALAD

It is proper to eat a salad using a knife and fork. A considerate hostess will tear the greens into bite-sized pieces.

SANDWICHES

Finger food. Unless they are opened-faced. Then you should use a knife and fork.

SHRIMP COCKTAIL

If the shrimp still has its tail or shell, then it is considered finger food. Anything else requires a cocktail fork. Please discard the tail or the shell on a plate.

SOFT-SHELL CRABS

Cut with a knife and fork into bite-sized sections and eat all of the crab.

SOUPS

The soup course is served in a bowl placed on a plate and eaten with a soup spoon. The soup spoon is pushed away from you towards the opposite side of the bowl, and then lifted to the mouth.

WATERMELON

Some eat watermelon with a fork. It can be a finger food if it is served in a ball.

LIST OF BASIC FINGER FOODS YOU CAN'T GO WRONG WITH

Bread
Carrot Sticks and Celery Stalks
Cheeses
Cookies
Corn on the Cob
Frankfurters
French Fries
Grapes
Hamburgers
Ice Cream on a stick
Nacho Chips
Pizza
Potato Chips
Sandwiches
Toast

"WHAT'S A FINGER BOWL?"

A finger bowl signals the end of the meal. It is a small dish of water with a slice of lemon or a flower floating in it. You dip your fingers in it, one hand at a time. For heaven sake, don't drink it! You are usually given a fresh napkin to dry your hands. Relax, you've made it. The meal is finished and you're out of the hot seat!

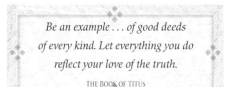

Be an example . . . of good deeds
of every kind. Let everything you do
reflect your love of the truth.

THE BOOK OF TITUS

CHAPTER EIGHT

Social Faux Pas

"DID YOU SEE WHAT THEY DID?"

*E*veryone has experienced the moment when you do something so unimaginably uncouth that you want to freeze time, sulk back to your house, and bury yourself deep behind all the clothes in your closet and hope that no one misses you ever again. These moments are common to all of us, though at the time it may feel like we're the only one who has ever made a mistake, or a social faux pas.

The best way to be sure of yourself in social settings is to become learned on the subject of social faux pas. The knowledge gathered below is your key to joining the rest of the world with your head held high and your pride and confidence soaring. After all, knowing is half the battle. It's up to you to do the rest. If, however, you ever do find yourself the culprit of a social faux pas, the key is to recover quietly and graciously. Refrain from drawing any more attention to yourself. Apologize and move on. That's all anyone really wants.

THE SECRET LIST OF SOCIAL FAUX PAS

POINTING

Pointing is in extremely bad taste and should be reserved only when you are forced to point out the guilty party from the witness stand in a courtroom.

SMOKING

Please refrain from smoking in someone's home or office. If they wanted their home or office to smell of smoke then they would set it on fire. Kindly step outside to smoke. And don't forget to clean up after yourself.

CHEWING GUM

Gum should be enjoyed in the privacy of your own home. Please, for the sake of the rest of us.

DRINKING LOUDLY WITH A STRAW

Avoid slurping by leaving a small amount of liquid in the bottom of your glass.

BREAKING IN LINE

Breaking in line is just simply rude and should not be done no matter where you are and that even includes your car!

LOUD MUSIC

Loud music is just a polite way to say noise pollution. Consider the other people around you. This is relevant from your home all the way to your car; especially in your car during bumper-to-bumper traffic.

UNWANTED OR ANNOYING TELEPHONE CALLS

It's amazing how invasive calls can be. Simply respond with a no thank you and hang up.

LACK OF MOVIE ETIQUETTE

Sit up and hush up. Unless you're tall, then slump down and be quiet. There are others that are interested in the movie. Also, eat popcorn with your mouth closed.

TALKING IN CHURCH

This is simply out of place. Save your talk until after the service and than have at it with your friends and family.

GOSSIP

Gossip is incredibly hurtful and always seems to get back to those it is about. Avoid it at all costs.

RACIAL OR ETHNIC JOKES

Racial or ethnic jokes or slurs are definitely unkind and in poor taste. Ethnic slang is never acceptable!

POOR HYGIENE

Poor hygiene is a reflection of a poor self-image. It is not respectful to yourself or to others.

ARGUING IN PUBLIC

It is embarrassing to others around you and should be extremely embarrassing to you.

TELLING PEOPLE OFF

Telling people off is the reaction of an immature, disrespectful person who does not possess the fine art of communication.

LEAVING A PARTY TOO SOON

It is rude and embarrassing when a guest leaves a party too soon. It makes it look like he wasn't having a good time. Don't get up from the table and leave until the meal is finished. A guest should be more considerate of his host's feelings.

LEAVING A PARTY TOO LATE

It is also embarrassing when a guest just doesn't get the clue that it's time to leave. The host is reduced to saying witty and veiled things like, "I think we're going to call it a night," or "I've got an early morning tomorrow." If you hear these things get out of there as soon as possible.

THE BULLY

The best thing to do is what your mother always told you to do when it comes to dealing with a bully—ignore him. Do not argue with him or try to change his attitude. Save your energy and just get up and leave.

LAUGHING AT AWKWARD TIMES

Laughing at inappropriate times is usually a nervous response from a person who is not comfortable in certain social situations. Work on this.

NERVOUS HABITS

Nervous habits, such as cracking your knuckles, biting your fingernails, or twirling your hair around your finger, are out of place. Try to discover what is making you uncomfortable and then work to change it.

WEARING HATS IN THE WRONG PLACES

If you wear hats in church or in other meeting places, consider those who cannot see through them. They may be pretty, but nothing can be that interesting for an hour.

PETS

Put pets up when a guest visits. They may not like your pets or your pets may not like them. Some people are allergic to cats and dogs.

CHILDREN IN THE WRONG PLACES

Don't subject children to adult places and situations. They're miserable and the more miserable they become, the more miserable you will be. It's a known fact. Examples of places that are not geared for children are restaurants that take a long time to seat or a wedding they are not directly invited to.

ACCIDENTS

It is terribly impolite to call attention to the mishaps that someone may cause. Accidents are just accidents and they happen sometimes. Handle the situation graciously by not using it as an opportunity to make fun of someone.

REST ROOM ETIQUETTE

Clean up after yourself and leave it fresh for the next person. Wipe up the sink area and pick up any paper towels you may have dropped.

BEING DISRESPECTFUL

Regardless of where you are, being disrespectful is never excusable.

WEARING SUNGLASSES INDOORS

They were named *sun*glasses for a reason. They are meant to shield your eyes from the glare of the sun.

CLEANING TEETH

Cleaning your teeth should be confined to your bathroom or the dentist's chair. Floss or brush your teeth in the privacy of your own home. Certainly, never use a toothpick at the table.

APPLYING MAKEUP

Rest room etiquette, please. Be sure to confine the powdering of your nose to the powder room. You may discreetly apply lipstick if you need to.

INTERRUPTING OTHERS

Rude. Rude. Rude. If you do it, there better be a really good reason why . . . like the house is on fire.

BEING NEGATIVE

A negative attitude is usually based on ignorance. Negative comments are a real downer. This attitude will cause people to flee from you.

WRONG IMPRESSIONS

Wrong impressions are wrong. Most of us form wrong impressions when we don't have all the facts or because we haven't spent enough time in a situation to know any different. The good thing is that wrong impressions are easily fixed.

OVEREATING AT A PARTY

Benjamin Franklin once advised that we should be careful to "eat to live and not live to eat." Overeating at a party is an act of selfishness and in poor taste, no pun intended.

TALKING WITH A MOUTHFUL OF FOOD

Wouldn't you be absolutely horrified if something fell out? Just a question.

MEN WHO DO NOT WAIT TO BE SEATED UNTIL AFTER WOMEN TAKE A SEAT

A swashbuckling pirate. Contrary to the movies, the pirate never ends up with the leading lady.

MEN WHO DO NOT OPEN A LADY'S CAR DOOR

It may seem an archaic practice, but opening the car door is an impressive way to show you care enough to treat your date with respect. It also shows your date that Prince Charming still does exist.

CRITICIZING FOOD

Never, ever do this at someone's home. You might as well tell them you think their dog is stupid and their cat has an attitude problem.

TOO MUCH PERFUME OR AFTER-SHAVE

Too much scent can be offensive to people who are allergic to strong fragrances. Save the bold ones for an evening at home.

OVER-COMPLIMENTING

Two words: Eddie Haskell. Over-complimenting is the most insincere form of flattery and is, underneath all the fancy sugar-coating, a lie.

BABY TALK

Grown people need to speak big people language. Leave the baby talk for those who really need it as their principle form of communication.

CANDLES BEING LIT BEFORE 6:00 P.M.

Candles should be lit only after six o'clock in the evening.

SALTING YOUR FOOD BEFORE YOU TASTE

This insults the hostess and is rude. Try the house version first, you might like it.

LIPSTICK ON YOUR GLASS

Lipstick on your glass has no class.

SLURPING YOUR SOUP

Stop and listen to yourself. If you can hear something then it means everyone else can too.

EATING BEFORE THE HOSTESS

Go ahead and try it. You may think it works, the first time. But there won't be a second time because you won't be invited back.

SNAPPING YOUR FINGERS TO GET THE ATTENTION OF THE WAITER

This is so crass, but it had to be included because we have witnessed this many times. Catch his eye or wave him down when he passes.

REACHING FOR FOOD

Ask for what you want instead. Consider it a covert way to make others do your bidding. Guess what, nobody will tell you no. And don't forget to say please.

ELBOWS ON THE TABLE

Can't you just hear your grandmother fussing at you?

LEAVING YOUR SPOON IN YOUR COFFEE CUP

When you have finished stirring your coffee, simply place your spoon on your saucer. Think of the saucer as a fancy spoon plate.

> *Three things in human life are important:*
> *The first is to be kind.*
> *The second is to be kind*
> *And the third is to be kind.*
>
> HENRY JAMES

PICKING UP YOUR DROPPED UTENSILS FROM THE FLOOR

In some countries, retrieving your dropped utensil might be a sign of deep respect and faith in your hostess' clean floor, but in the U.S., just ask for another.

LEANING BACK IN YOUR CHAIR

You might find it relaxing. You might even think it makes you look somewhat cool in a distant sort of way, but how cool will you look if the chair falls backward? Play it safe, sit up straight.

DON'T PUSH YOUR PLATE AWAY FROM YOU AFTER YOU EAT

This is rude. To your hostess, it looks like you don't want to be close to her food any longer than you absolutely have to.

DON'T SLOUCH IN YOUR CHAIR

You should have learned this as a child, but if you didn't, learn it now.

BLOWING YOUR NOSE WITH YOUR NAPKIN

Gross and terribly unacceptable at the table. Excuse yourself and go to the rest room.

PUTTING ON AIRS

Putting on airs will always backfire on you. Once a girl from Ann's hometown went to England and came back with an English accent . . . no comment.

GETTING UP FROM THE TABLE BEFORE YOUR HOSTESS RISES

Getting up from the table before your hostess is ill-mannered. You may leave the table only if you have to be excused to go to the rest room.

TELLING DIRTY JOKES

Crude, rude, and will definitely not land you many dates.

TELLING TRAGIC STORIES
Leave this to the television networks.

TALKING ABOUT PHYSICAL AILMENTS
This should only be for your physician's ears or your attorney's.

STARING
This is something you should have stopped doing in the first grade. If you still do it, do not pass go, do not collect two hundred dollars, and go directly to jail.

EAVESDROPPING
Eavesdropping is a first cousin to gossiping. Their whole family should be scratched from your address book.

FIGHTING OVER PAYING THE BILL
This is so not necessary. Fighting over the bill is equivalent to flexing your muscles.

CORRECTING OTHERS
Correcting others is a show of arrogance. No one appreciates being corrected. Besides, you may not be right.

SHOUTING
Shouting indicates someone who is a poor communicator. By shouting, you invade someone else's air space.

NOT HOLDING THE DOOR OPEN FOR THE NEXT PERSON
Inconsiderate and self-centered. Besides, you may need that person to hold the door open for you someday. Kindness has a way of popping back up again.

NOT GIVING UP YOUR SEAT TO AN OLDER PERSON
Think of what your grandmother would say. Better yet, picture your grandmother being forced to stand.

BORROWING FROM OTHERS AND NOT RETURNING
Bad, really bad. Neither a borrower nor a lender be.

LOSING YOUR TEMPER

See a counselor and learn self-control.

ASKING TOO MANY PERSONAL QUESTIONS

This really invades someone's private space. It's like an interrogation.

BREAKING A DATE (UNLESS IT IS AN ABSOLUTE EMERGENCY)

Remember the little boy who cried wolf? You're not in danger of being consumed by a wolf, but people may stop inviting you places.

ASSUMING WHAT ANOTHER PERSON IS THINKING

If you can figure out what is in the mind of someone else, we need to take this act on the road.

BEING RUDE TO YOUR HOSTESS

Could you maybe think of anything else more stupid? If you do this, you probably need to stay at home by yourself!

STAYING TOO LONG AFTER YOUR MEAL AT A RESTAURANT

They want to seat others and this throws them off when you do this. Leave within five minutes after the meal.

RUNNING UP A HUGE BILL AT A RESTAURANT OR CLUB AT YOUR HOST'S EXPENSE

This is another winner! Stay in the mid-range.

GOING TO A RESTAURANT WITHOUT ENOUGH MONEY OR A CREDIT CARD AND RELYING, INSTEAD, ON YOUR FRIENDS TO TAKE CARE OF YOUR PART

Your friends should make you wash the dishes!

CONFRONTING PEOPLE TO TELL THEM IT'S YOUR TURN

Step aside. Let them go first. It's not worth the negative effort.

CHAPTER NINE

Thank You Very Much

"FROM MERCI BEAUCOUP TO GRACI"

*P*eople do nice things for us each day and deserve to be thanked. Thanking someone is an incredibly small detail that can make someone feel unbelievably wonderful and appreciated. It makes for joy in the little things we do each day, both for ourselves and others.

THE ALPHABET OF THE THANK-YOU NOTE

You name it, we got it. The ins and outs of thank-you notes begin with the supplies you'll need. It's really quite simple and it will just take a moment of your time. The following represent the basic types of stationery:

FOLDOVER CARDS

Foldover cards are for writing informal notes. They usually measure 4" x 5" when folded and have matching envelopes. You may have your initials monogrammed on the very top of the front page and your return address printed on the back flap of the envelope.

> *People will listen a great deal more*
> *patiently while you explain your mistakes*
> *Than when you explain your successes.*
>
> WILBUR N. NESBIT

PERSONAL STATIONERY

Personal stationery is used for letter writing. The individual sheets measure 7" x 9" and quite often include the sender's full name, address, and phone number at the very top of the letter sheet. After the first sheet, additional sheets are blank and do not bear the sender's name and address. Matching envelopes are for a one-third fold. It is quite acceptable for a single woman to list just her address and not include her name on the back flap of the envelope.

The road to the heart
is the ear.

VOLTAIRE

Suzzana Holmes
254 Mockingbird Place
Decatur, Georgia 30030

Suzzana Holmes
254 Mockingbird Place
Decatur, Georgia 30030

BUSINESS STATIONERY

Business stationery is stationery for business writing. Yes, even in the business world thank-you notes are necessary. Business sheets measure 8 1/2" x 11" and appear with the name, address, and phone number printed at the top of the page. Matching No. 10 envelopes are for a one-third fold. It is acceptable for business stationery to carry a more elaborate corporate logo or to list, for example, the names of their Board of Directors.

Some say that the age of chivalry is past,
that the spirit of romance is dead. The age of chivalry
is never past, so long as there is a wrong left
unredressed on earth, or a man or woman left to say:
"I will redress that wrong,
or spend my life in the attempt."
CHARLES KINGSLEY

ANN PLATZ & CO.
FIVE PIEDMONT CENTER
ATLANTA, GEORGIA 30305

ANN PLATZ & CO.
FIVE PIEDMONT CENTER
ATLANTA, GEORGIA 30305

POST CARDS

Post cards are ideal for dropping quick notes to people. They measure 4" x 6" on a heavy card. Usually this card is printed with a colored border and the sender's name only at the top. These can be sent in matching envelopes.

Morals refine manners,
as manners refine morals.

MARIE VON EBNER-ESCHENBACH

Margaret Williams

MEMO PADS

Memo pads are perfect for jotting down quick notes (usually in lieu of sending a longer letter or cover letter). Anywhere from one-third to half of a page in size, the sender's name usually appears on the bottom of the pad. It is often considered tacky and out of place if you use the phrase "From the desk of" or "Things to do." Keep it simple. Let the note speak louder than the notepad.

There's always a best way of doing everything, if it be to boil an egg. Manners are the happy ways of doing things.

RALPH WALDO EMERSON

Memo

Susan Wales

BORROWING STATIONERY

When traveling, one of things we usually forget to pack is stationary. Often, it is just easier to use the stationery that your hotel provides. If this is the case, write "as from" below the letterhead and then add your appropriate address.

GREETING CARDS

It is always preferable to handwrite notes inside greeting cards. No greeting card company can ever accomplish what you can when you speak from your heart. Take the time and it will be appreciated.

Of course, there are many instances where prewritten, mass-produced greeting cards not only come in handy, but also prove necessary. Businesses quite often send out these mass greeting cards to promote special events, offers, or simply thank their customers and clients. If your company does send out prewritten cards, it would be wonderfully nice if you could include a handwritten note. This says that you make time to take care of even the tiniest details. Remember: Ladies first! A lady always signs her name first. For example: "Ann and John Platz."

LETTER WRITING ON THE COMPUTER

Write formal letters only by hand. Personal letters may be typed on the computer. It's even become acceptable to either e-mail or fax this typed letter. But truthfully, it's a tough call. Although speedier, and sometimes easier to read than handwritten letters, something intangibly human is taken out of the entire affair. It remains preferable to handwrite, but a computer letter is better than no letter.

WHAT'S IN A NAME?

A business letter is signed with a person's full name unless there exists a more informal relationship between the sender and recipient. But in the case of those you do not really know, the full signature is the appropriate way of identifying yourself to a business contact.

Married women should sign a business letter with the name under which they conduct business. If signing a business letter that is from both her and her husband she should include her married name as well.

Personal letters should of course be signed just with your first name. They are called personal letters for a reason.

WHY MIXING AND MATCHING IS A BAD IDEA

There is an old adage that advises us against mixing business with pleasure. This holds true even in regard to letter writing. It is terribly inappropriate to either mix your personal and business stationery or use one in the place of the other. Using business correspondence automatically creates a sense of distance and makes it clear to the person you're writing to that you do not think of the relationship on anything other than business terms. Also, never have your secretary or assistant write or type your personal correspondence. This really distances you from whomever you are writing to. Take the time to make it personal. Keep business separate from your personal life and vice versa.

Never respond to a letter by simply adding to it in the margins. Reply to a letter with a separate letter. This again demonstrates your interest in the other person and their business with you.

THE BREAD AND BUTTER NOTE

You may tell your hostess thank you as you leave the party, but you will still need to write a thank-you note. This is called a "bread and butter" note. It should be written on personal stationery. The note should be addressed to the hostess and should thank both her and her spouse. An example would be the following:

> *Dear Susan,*
>
> *John and I enjoyed our lovely dinner with you and Ken last evening. You are a marvelous hostess and tremendous cook! I will call you soon to set a date for both of you to join us for dinner at our home.*
>
>

Sincerely,

Ann

If you have been honored as the guest of honor at a dinner, please send written thanks immediately.

RSVP ASAP: RESPONDING TO THE RSVP AND REGRETS ONLY

Upon receiving an invitation with an RSVP, you should reply immediately. An RSVP informs the hostess whether or not you are planning to attend the upcoming function. In addition to informing her of your attendance, an RSVP also gives her a total number of those who will be coming. Today many hostesses will list *regrets only* instead of RSVP. Regrets only requires the guest to respond only if they are *not* attending.

ACCEPTING AN INVITATION

In an acceptance you should repeat the information given in the original invitation. A formal RSVP must be done

*Fine manners need the support
of fine manners in others.*

RALPH WALDO EMERSON

in writing and then sent to the hostess. By doing this, you ensure that there has been no miscommunication. If you are writing a regret, you should also include much of the same information. The same may be done for a response to an informal invitation. It is also perfectly acceptable to respond to an informal invitation over the phone.

A formal response:

Dear Mrs. Smithart:
Mr. Davis and I will be thrilled to join you
and Mr. Smithart at the Ritz Hotel for dinner on
Thursday, April 12, at 8 o'clock. We look forward
to the occasion.
                    Sincerely,
                        Maria Davis

An informal response:

Dear Marjorie,
Thank you so much for your thoughtful invitation
to Mitchell's fortieth birthday party for Saturday,
November 20. Harold and I look forward to seeing
you both at three o'clock at the Marina.
                    Sincerely,
                        Meredith

ACKNOWLEDGING GIFTS, CARDS, AND DEEDS

It is wonderful and encouraging to thank someone in person. Yet it is also important to thank them in writing. This shows the person that you appreciated their kindness or gesture so much that you went home and thought about it. You should write them immediately.

CHAPTER TEN

Social Graces

"THEY ARE MORE THAN JUST THE RULES"

Dear Friends,

Well, we've come a long way, haven't we? We hope these social graces have helped you. Just a few more words and then it'll be time to turn you loose. We'll send you on to spread your wings and fly away.

Remember that life is meant to be enjoyed. It is a gift and we all must choose how we want to use it. We all should feel incredible joy and abundance each day. We are also meant to share this gift with others. Knowing and understanding the social graces is a way to ensure that this happens.

In life, rules can only take you so far. The rules that have been set out in this book are here to act as a starting point. It is up to you to work past these and to grow and love on your own. No book can teach you how to do that. But what this book can show you, or begin to show you, is that living requires much more than simply playing by the rules. Living requires social grace.

There are just some lessons you absolutely need to learn before you can move forward. One of these lessons is how to treat others. Boiled right down to the point, *Social Graces* teaches you how to respond to all situations and all people with love, patience, kindness, and always with an open heart full of joy. You can master which fork to use with what course and the proper way to handle introductions, but what remains is that the real lesson is the importance of radiating love to all you meet, no matter who, no matter where, no matter when.

Social graces are how we choose to handle ourselves and are our tools in unearthing the wonderful and peaceful beauty that resides in all of us. These graces show up in the little things we do, or should do, everyday: Smile and say hello, hold the door open for someone else, be considerate of others, and show each other that we do see and hear each other. It's amazing that such little things can bring such great happiness to everyone involved.

Manners are universal and are the very epitome of human interaction. From the beaches of Southern California to the busy streets of New York and from the changing leaves of Vermont all the way to the heart of the Deep South, we could all use some good talkin' to when it comes to manners and politeness.

> *I describe not men, but manners;*
> *not an individual but a species.*
>
> HENRY FIELDING

A Word from the Artist . . .

When Ruth Samsel, a gem from Harvest House Publishers, asked me to paint the artwork for Social Graces *I prayed for divine confirmation, for my heart was dedicated to painting children. Confirmation came boldly when I reviewed the manuscript and realized that Ann Platz was one of the writers. Ann was the first to represent my artwork ten years ago and she encouraged me to take my artwork from a hobby to a profession.*

Our reunion today is a harvest from seeds of character and good manners that were planted yesterday. I deeply appreciate Ann Platz, Susan Wales, and Harvest House Publishers for their vision in recognizing the importance of Social Graces. *I thank my family, generations past and present, for teaching me the precious value of family, church, and community. Since I am a representative for each of these, it's manners—my manners— that holds me to a higher standard.*

Kathy Fincher

Acknowledgments

We would like to thank our wonderful husbands,

John Platz and Ken Wales

for their constant love, encouragement, advice and support throughout this project.

A grateful thank you to Ruth Samsel, our editor at Harvest House, for her guidance and enthusiasm. And to the fantastic team at Harvest House, especially Barbara Sherrill and Kim Moore, we owe our deep appreciation. And for the beautiful artwork without which this book would be incomplete we thank Kathy Fincher. A huge thank you to the wonderful design firm of Koechel Peterson & Associates who put this book together. For their expertise and dedication, we thank Angelina McCormick and Kim Lewis.

To the reader, we hope you will laugh and smile as we grow together in the social graces.

With love and devotion this book is dedicated to the dearest and loveliest of parents, Mr. and Mrs. Arthur Joseph Huey, Jr., whose inner beauty surpasses all! You not only gave me the precious gift of life but also, by your impeccable example, love, faith, kindness, and generosity. This book is for all the times I rolled my eyes when you said, "Pretty is as pretty does!" And as a parent myself, I know you've both waited a long time for a thank-you for making me mind my manners . . . Thank you!

To my grandparents, Mr. and Mrs. Arthur J. Huey, Sr. and Mr. and Mrs. George R. Benefield, whose Sunday dinners not only taught me manners, but love of family and more about life than I could have imagined! And a special thanks to my late in-laws Dr. and Mrs. Wales Smith and their parents for teaching your son, my husband Ken Wales, the most beautiful social graces I've ever seen in a man!

And a special hug to my daughter, Meg Chrane, whose patience and understanding is endearing!

Susan Wales

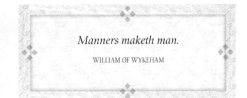

Manners maketh man.

WILLIAM OF WYKEHAM